CONQUERING HEARTBREAK

A PERSONAL GUIDE
THROUGH THE WILDERNESS
OF LOVE-LOSS

D. D. Thompson

Published by Thompson Consulting Inc.
Crane, St. Philip, Barbados

Edited by G. A. Murray
Designed by Caribbean Chapters Publishing Inc.

ISBN (paperback): 978-976-95923-0-8

Dedication

All Praise and Thanks to God
through whom ALL things are possible.

To my mother Janice: you are my inspiration.

To my daughter Naleena: though I pray you will
never need this book, break-ups are a natural part
of life. To my son Khaden: thank you for keeping
me company many nights as I wrote.

And to you, dear reader, even if my advice is not
helpful at all, I hope reading this book provides a
temporary distraction, and that your laughing at
my experiences lightens your mood.

To all the guys who have broken my heart: this
book is dedicated to **ME!**

A CONQUEROR!

"The Lord is close to the broken hearted
and saves those who are crushed in spirit."

Psalm 34:18 NIV

Table of Contents

Foreword

Conquering Heartbreak is simple and down to earth. If you're looking for 10 ways to get back at your Ex you won't find them in this book. Thompson takes a mature, candid and realistic look at the emotional trauma that characterises break-ups. She intersperses it with sound words of wisdom and, in her inimitable style, splashes of humour, as if to remind the reader that this too will pass. The book climaxes with some potent advice and tips on how to pick the pieces up and move on to new beginnings. A must-read for all who have been on the roller coaster of bad relationships and have not yet figured out how to begin the healing process, and for those who are still there, and are desperately looking for a way to disembark.

Cora Jordan

important to know and believe that heartbreak is not a fatal condition. You will get over it. How soon and how completely depends entirely on **You**.

I hope and pray that you find this book useful in your own healing process.

ONE

The End

HOW IRONIC that we should begin at the end. Ironic, but apt. The first thing I absolutely recommend that you do is to be fully persuaded in your own mind that the relationship is indeed over, with no possibility of reconciliation. This is the first step towards recovery. Once you know for sure that it is over, do not second-guess yourself. Mentally come to grips with the fact that **it is** over and accept it. Because it is over- finished- done- caput- finito- history. Your heart, unfortunately, is much tougher to convince.

Our past experiences and background play a significant role in how we react when we encounter conflict in a relationship. We can sometimes blow a minor infraction completely out of proportion, ending a good relationship for trivial reasons, only to spend years regretting our hasty actions. Or, we can sweep major issues under the carpet because we value the facade of a relationship more than we value ourselves. Or other times we can stay in a relationship long past its "best before date", spending so much time looking back at what once was, that we are unable to see what now is.

"The Only Thing That is Constant is Change"

– Heraclitus –

This maxim is especially true in the case of relationships. As time passes, your feelings towards your significant other will inevitably change. The problem arises however, when in a relationship, the feelings of each party differ drastically from the other: One person is falling deeper in love and the other person is desperately trying to escape.

Sometimes those first, fluttery stirrings of the heart at the beginning of a romance solidify, growing deeper and stronger in intensity, ending in "happily ever after". Sometimes, after the initial hazy fog of infatuation through which we see our sweetheart evaporates, the person we now see is not so desirable after all. Some personality traits and behaviours of your love-muffin which once warmed your heart, now gall you to the core. That helpless trait in your partner which you found so innocent and endearing when you first met, now comes over as weakness. Where you once felt needed, you now feel burdened. Instead of feeling appreciated, you feel used. Assertive now becomes pushy and bombastic, and protective is now judged as jealous and controlling.

Other times the relationship is perfect, until one party does or says something that hurts, degrades or embarrasses the other person. If there is no discussion, resolution or forgiveness, a rift develops. Just enough space for resentment or outside influences to invade, and soon enough your rift has developed into a chasm. Captain! Rough seas ahead! If only we had the courage to communicate openly and honestly at all times with each other. If only we had the strength and maturity to hear and accept the truth when offered.

Long after your partner has emotionally "checked-out" of the relationship, you may be aware but unwilling to let go, like me.

Seth had grown increasing distant. When I asked him what was wrong, predictably he said, "Nothing". But I didn't buy it. Panicked and confused, I dug my heels in deeper. I reasoned that if I could only love him better, I could recapture his attention and affection. I turned up the "sweet" and amped up the "passion": Back rubs, home cooked meals, spontaneous gifts, thoughtful gestures, and a steady diet of sex were the order of the day. But as the weeks went by the "nothing" was intensifying, and instead of recapturing Seth, I started to lose myself. The anxiety and turmoil I felt whenever we were apart; the abandonment when he didn't call or when he broke a date; the loneliness I suffered being with someone who though physically present, was emotionally light years away; feeling devalued and empty for having given my heart, body and soul away without reciprocity. My self-worth eventually packed up and left. Seth left soon afterwards.

I learned two valuable lessons from this experience:

Preface

For the purpose of this book, "heartbreak" is defined as the feeling of loss, sadness or rejection experienced when a romantic relationship ends or "breaks up". Though the causes of break-ups are several and diverse, they are usually signalled when one or both parties in a relationship have indicated either verbally or otherwise, that they no longer wish to be a part of that union. This book attempts to chart a course through the churning, terrifying waters of heartbreak to calmer seas and brighter skies.

Break-ups are hard. I would know. I've had enough of them. No matter how or why they occur, the end result is the same. Pain. Intense gut-wrenching pain. A hollow feeling in the stomach that comes from deep loss and resulting emptiness. Should the end be abrupt and unexpected, the pain is sharp and piercing; constricting the lungs, throwing the mind into total confusion. Other times there is a long, winding descent into a nothingness ending. That pain is just as intense, but with more of a throbbing ache that extends from the heart in waves and touches every organ and system of the body.

Whether sudden or expected, eventually with all endings other emotions come to the party: anger directed at the "offending" party; doubt as to if the break-up was a mistake or if more could have been done to salvage the relationship; fear of being alone; resentment at being alone after investing so much in the relationship. This resentment is intensified, especially if the other party seems to have easily moved on with their own life without you. Emptiness from having a huge gap in your life, the vacated space and time that person once occupied.

Whether it is your second, third, or thirty-third heartbreak, this in no way defines who you are, or your ability to be in a successful relationship in the future. These bumps along life's road make us stronger and wiser, and teach us valuable lessons about human nature; about what love is, and what love is not. In fact, I challenge you to deny that you cannot fully appreciate a good partner unless you have had a bad one.

During the whole recovery period, it is most

1. Sometimes when someone has made up their mind to leave a relationship, there isn't anything you can do to make them stay.
2. Your love should never be used as a bribe, ransom, blackmail, consolation, bargaining chip, weapon, yoke or fetter.

I have also been on the other side of this unequal equation. Trying so hard to feel something for somebody who was doing everything they could to win back my affections. Seeing the fear, and pain, and desperation in his eyes, and knowing I was the cause, made me feel unfairly burdened and guilty - desperate to get away. In these situations, there are no winners; only two miserable losers. Love and life, neither of them is fair.

There are some relationships which don't even meet the basic criteria for being called one. Sometimes lonely and desperate, we take our "What I am looking for in a mate" list, toss it out the window and latch on to the first person who even looks like they are looking in our direction. We shut out the voice in our heads which seeks to steer us clear of danger, warning us of the car wreck which lies ahead, and instead run merrily headlong to our demise.

When these unions end, we can spend a very long time chiding and blaming ourselves for making such bad decisions. Experience is said to be the greatest teacher, and wisdom comes from learning from our experiences. As we grow in wisdom, we are expected to be better able then to handle similar situations differently in the future, or better yet, avoid such situations altogether. However, in the midst of the highly emotive confusion and pain of a relationship in trouble, we can lose the ability to draw rational conclusions and make sound decisions. When I have found myself in such a muddled state, I found it useful to employ one of two methods to help me determine if a relationship was worth holding onto or letting go.

The first is a very simple analytical tool called the "Pros and Cons List".

To do this, take a sheet of paper and draw a line down the middle, thereby creating two columns. On the top of the first column write the word "Pros" and on top of the second column write "Cons". Then under the appropriated headings, list the pros and cons of the relationship.

Here is a sample of the Pros and Cons list I made

just before the end of my relationship with Drew.

Pros	Cons
	1. My emotional needs not being met
	2. He doesn't share his feelings with me
	3. He trivialises my concerns
	4. Relationship not growing or deepening
	5. He unapologetically ogles other women and flirts openly

After much soul-searching I was unable to come up with any Pros; nothing recent anyhow. There in black and white, the sad truth emerged. It was over.

The second tool is going to sound a bit bizarre at first, but it certainly worked for me when I had to make a really difficult decision to end a relationship gone wrong, which used to be oh so right.

Long after I should have closed the final chapter on 'The Life and Times of Akeem and

I", we were still together – sort of. It was the classic case of an immovable object meeting an irresistible force. I was the marrying kind and Akeem was not. We were at that age where most of our friends were making this ultimate commitment to each other, and with each wedding we attended, the more cold, distant, irrational and ridiculous Akeem behaved – like a condemned man whose appointment with the gallows was fast approaching. It got to the stage where he no longer introduced me as his girlfriend. I was now only my first and last name. His theatrics had the desired effect, as I became so frustrated and disgusted by his childish behaviour, that there was not the slightest chance I would have ever agreed to marry him, even if he asked. And so it begged the question: "Why were we still together at all?" It was time to convene a Management Meeting, with myself.

Are you facing similar circumstances? I suggest that this meeting be called to order in the privacy of your room, while staring at yourself squarely in the eyes in the mirror. As CEO, sternly but lovingly remind yourself of your core values and goals in life, and the qualities and attributes you desire in a mate. Next, as Inventory Manager, expound on your talents and strengths. Be honest as well about your weaknesses. As Finance Manager, confront yourself with this pivotal question: "Does your income match your expenditure?" In other words, do the benefits of being in the relationship outweigh the compromises? Are you getting as much as you are giving? At this point in my high level meeting, my Human Resources manager reminded me that there was nothing wrong with seeking a promotion for which I believed I was qualified. In fact, holding the position of "girlfriend" when I really desired to be a "wife", in a relationship where no such vacancy existed, was the source of my frustrations. The Sales Manager then worked with me to re-define my "brand". I had grown and changed over the years and, as expected, so had my needs and desires. There was no need to feel badly about this, as it was a natural part of life. People in relationships change. Sometimes they grow together and sometimes they grow apart.

If, for whatever reason, you are still unsure that the relationship is completely over, ask yourself the following questions:

- Is reconciliation desirable?
- Is the other party open to working to fix what is wrong with the relationship?
- Is it unlikely that the circumstances which led to the breakup will recur?

If you answered "Yes" to any of these, put this book down and come back when you know for sure that the relationship is over. Do not be embarrassed by this seeming indecision. Most of us have all been in situations we were convinced were over, only to make up ten minutes later, fully apologetic, reaffirming our undying love and commitment and all the other wonderful things that come with breaking-up and making-up.

I believe though, that **deep down we know for sure when a relationship is over**. When we know we have gone around the same mountain for the last time. Going around in circles is fine if you are running track, or moving on the dance floor. Going around in life circles simply does not indicate progress and only serves to make us emotionally dizzy.

Let me explain what I mean by going around the same mountain.

Anthony was a sneak. Half-truths and omissions were his native language. I realised this when in recounting any story or experience he had, the latest version always varied from the one before. I am not talking about little details like what colour shirt he was wearing at the time or what time of the day it occurred. I mean in major ways like: "Today (Friday) was a quiet day at work thanks for asking"; to "Last Friday I was a few minutes late getting back from lunch and my boss really let me have it"; and "One Friday last month I ran into my 'Ex' at lunch and we chatted so long it was hours before I got back to work." I would get angry, accuse him of being a liar and declare that I didn't trust him. He of course didn't "understand" what I was acting so crazy about. He would counter that I got upset at every little thing, which is why he sometimes kept things from me so we wouldn't argue. He hated arguments. It never occurred to him that had he told the whole truth at the start, there would be no need for an argument down the road. This pattern of secrets and revelations led to my having very little, if any, trust in him. All of his stories ended with me initially interrogating him just to make sure all the salient details were extracted (which never happened anyway), which led to his saying I didn't trust him, and him hiding even more to avoid the inevitable argument. This would always lead to one of us emphatically stating, "I can't go on like this!" But after a few days of strained relations, we would profess we couldn't live without each other. We were stuck in a loop of: I love you. You're a liar/crazy. It's over. (Repeat). Stuck in this holding pattern, it was inevitable that we would run out of emotional fuel and be forced to make an emergency landing.

If it is over, accept that it is. Do not foster any hope of reconciling. **Hope in this situation is not your friend.** It only serves to prolong the hurt, leave you vulnerable and retard the healing process. Accept that he was not "The One", or you would not need this book to begin with, would you?

Very often, the very next day, or a few days or weeks in the aftermath of the break-up, there will be a strong temptation to contact the other party. Not being able to withstand the knee-buckling hurt, we may make up in our minds to call and beg for the relationship to be given another try, to change their minds. This would be a fatal error.

Such begging results in the other party either:

1. Crushing your feelings further by answering "No", thus doubling your feelings of rejection, added to which will be the humiliation of begging someone to take you back, with the attempt being an utter failure; or

2. Taking you back because they either feel sorry for you or because they do not have the guts to say what is truly in their heart, namely "NO!"

Should there be "reconciliation", this usually leads to another break-up soon after, or a type of emotional blackmail. Since you were the person who begged to be taken back, you now have to accept any conditions or horrible treatment imposed. After all, you begged for it. Unless both parties are fully committed to honestly working at repairing the relationship, begging for another chance curtails your progress towards healing and takes you back to the beginning again – The End.

I remember when it ended with Dave. Honesty was not his strong suit and consequently I had deep trust issues – All the necessary ingredients for fiery arguments. Trust, being at the helm of any relationship, it was no wonder our love boat listed, took on water and began to sink. After abandoning ship, the pain was too much for me and a few weeks later I begged him to throw me a lifeline, to reconsider. He agreed. He spent about six months reconsidering, all the while enjoying all the benefits of a relationship without any of the constraints, compromises or sacrifices. He was free to see me or not, spend time with whomever he pleased. I had painted myself into a tight corner because I wanted him back. I had to eventually cut myself free from the string from which he had me dangling and start again at the end. Had I accepted *it was over the first time, six months on I would have been over him completely.*

Researcher Dr. Brian Boutwell, an associate professor of epidemiology at Saint Louis University in the USA, analysed studies about break-ups and love with a focus on evolutionary psychology. Results from MRI scans showed an increase in neuronal activity in the parts of the brain - the pleasure areas - that also become active with cocaine use. Dr Boutwell said falling out of love might be compared to asking a cocaine addict to break his or her habit, adding: *"To sever that bond and move on is a huge ask of a person. Ultimately, trying to move on from a former mate may be similar in some ways to an attempt at breaking a drug habit."*

Unfortunately, I have experienced this first-hand.

Ryan was like cocaine of the highest grade. Mesmerised by his incredible good looks and physical perfection, it was lust at first sight. He was also charming, funny and showered me with attention. Ryan had the magical ability to make even mundane activities, like washing the dishes, seem fun and exciting. But when it came to important issues like shared interests, long-term goals, values, and handling of finances, or sharing thoughts and feelings, I was Venus and he was Mars.

Though we hardly had anything in common, his love-making abilities more than compensated for all other deficiencies in our relationship. At least that is what I told myself at the time. I was caught in the gravitational pull of his heavenly body, and after my first "hit", I was a shameless addict. It wasn't long before all of our encounters were strictly physical. Our relationship was emotionally shallow, physically exhausting and mentally retarding; devoid of any real substance; just a bad "habit".

My brain was telling me I had to end it, but none of my other body parts agreed. On my first serious attempt to end the "relationship", I took great pains to explain to Ryan what I needed and what I wasn't getting in our relationship. He listened quietly then picked me up in his arms, kissed me with those warm soft lips, and took me to the bedroom. Score-Ryan 1: Me 0. On my second attempt, I told him I didn't want to see him anymore, to just leave me alone. Fifteen minutes later, Ryan was standing in my doorway, smelling and looking good enough to eat. My steely resolve to resist his charms was as useless as a bikini in a blizzard. Score- Ryan 2: Me 0. I fought valiantly to break my "habit". I ignored his calls and refused to answer the door when he came by. Then Ryan sent one of his "special" selfies to my mobile phone. Ten minutes later I was frantically pressing his doorbell and he answered the door wearing only a smile. Score- Ryan 3, 4 & 5: Me, 0. Four months on Ryan's score continued to tick over at a steady pace. Mine sadly never made it above 5.

When I finally said goodbye to Ryan for the very last time, I thought I would die. Thankfully, Dr Boutwell's research findings proved to be true.

According to Dr. Boutwell, *"Our review of the literature suggests we have a mechanism in our brains designed by natural selection to pull us through a very tumultuous time in our lives...it suggests people will recover; the pain will go away with time. There will be a light at the end of the tunnel."*

So be encouraged, even science proves that you will get over your heartbreak.

- Accept that the relationship is over.
- Do not hold out hope for a reconciliation
- Be resolute, no turning back.
- Science proves that you will get over your heartbreak.

Now breathe a sigh of relief. The madness is at an end. Let the healing begin.

Notes

TWO

Disentanglement

AT THIS MOST vulnerable time, you may feel that the only person who can "fix" your broken heart is the one who broke it in the first place. You imagine that with just the right words or the right gestures, the pieces of your fragmented heart would miraculously come together and be made whole. You believe that maintaining some sort of contact with the person would soften the impact, dampen the blow. However, this contact may be more harmful than helpful. If seeing or hearing the person leaves you feeling worse instead of better, I strongly urge you to **consider severing all ties**.

Whatsapp, Twitter, Instagram, Facebook, Linkedin, Instant Messaging. In this technological age, where we are always plugged into other people's lives through social media, it can be particularly challenging to avoid others. This will call for a level of thoroughness, decisiveness and blunt brutality to which you may be unaccustomed. Never mind though, practice makes perfect. For example, in the case of your Facebook account, deleting that person from your "Friends" list may not do the job completely. Other friends may have to go as well, especially if they are in the habit of posting events, photos or news threads which have your Ex tagged in them. The reason for this is simple.

You do not want to be constantly bombarded by a stream of information and updates about your Ex's life and you do not wish him to have easy access to the details of yours. You do not want to be tempted to re-establish contact or let your heart be dragged through the mud by following his exciting life on Instagram. Wounds tend to heal faster if they are left alone and not constantly poked and picked at. Your heart is in intensive care, on life support. Visitors are through necessity restricted at this time to close family and a few friends. Do not feel guilty in any way about cutting some people off. **You are in self-preservation mode**. Retreat to your safe place and tend to your wounds.

- Block.
- Delete.
- Unfriend.
- Unfollow.

Sharing the sordid details of your current situation on social media is a definite no-no. No changing of status from "in a relationship" to "single". No posts bashing the other party or divulging sensitive information or embarrassing photos. Have some self-respect otherwise you will only leave yourself open to ridicule, gossip and pity. This juvenile behaviour has the potential to escalate into something destructive, especially if the other person decides to give you tit for tat. Just graciously and quietly slip into the background, for now.

If your Ex chooses to indulge in this behaviour or if word reaches you that he has been spreading lies about you, suppress the urge to react similarly. You have no control over what he does; **you have**

control only over your own actions. Tell yourself that he is crying out for attention like a child throwing a tantrum. Do not reward him by getting caught up in his melodrama. As does every good parent who has had a child in the candy aisle of the supermarket, spread-eagled on the floor, bawling and creating a scene, disown him, step over him and walk away.

- No juvenile behaviour.
- Do not reward tantrums.

Incredibly, sometimes after a break-up, your new Ex may request to remain friends. You may be tempted to say yes; after all, how could it hurt? You may believe this "friends" offer to be just the lifeline you need to somehow lessen the impact of a complete break, and secretly you may hope that this would lead to every jilted lover's dream of getting back together. Before you make your decision, I will tell you what I discovered about remaining friends with an Ex. **In many instances, you were never friends to begin with.** To try now to make an ex-lover into a friend is like trying to make a proverbial silk purse from a sow's ear. And I should know, I tried it once.

I soon realised what "remaining friends" really meant to James. He could call me when he needed a favour and ignore my calls when he didn't need anything. He could drop by if he was bored, get comfortable, make it feel like old times and then remind me that I had no claims on him when I asked when I would see him again. He could tell me all about his new love interest and get advice on how to impress her, regardless of how much it crushed my heart. And I couldn't complain because friends were supposed to look out for, and be happy for each other. He could take me on a guilt trip because I actually had a life, or no time or desire to bolster his ego if he needed to talk.

This illusion of being friends keeps your wound open and sucks the remaining emotional life out of you. And worst of all, with emotions being so raw and human nature being what it is, you may make the fatal error of fooling yourself that you are back together, or worse yet, beg to get back together. **Sever all ties, until you can see the** person or hear them, or hear about them and feel *nothing*. No hurt, no anger, just plain nothing. This prevents regression.

Just trust me on this one.

Do not talk about the person, or try to do so as seldom as possible. You are not ready for this yet. Pretend they are dead. Discourage your friends from bringing you "news" about the person, no matter how juicy. He is no longer your concern. Your only concern is you. He is dead, remember? **Instead of remaining friends, my advice is this: avoid, Avoid, AVOID!**

Avoid the person, mutual friends, places, things, anything connected to, or which reminds you of the person. PUT AWAY ALL photos, clothes, underwear, greeting cards, gifts, movie stubs, love notes... everything that is connected directly to that person. **Do not** look at them. This will only set back your progress.

- If you were not friends before, don't try to become friends after.
- Pretend the person is dead.
- Discourage news bringers (they can also be news carriers).

I also strongly advise against trespassing on

your Ex's territory. Do not turn up at his place unannounced, pretending to return some item of his that he left at your place or demanding some insignificant trinket back. Do not skulk around the court where he plays basketball or join his health club knowing full well you are allergic to exercise. And for heaven's sake, do not be so silly as to show up at an event to which you were both invited before the split. Do not call his home and hang up just to see who will answer the phone. Do not wait outside his place to see who enters or leaves. This is called stalking. There is nothing flattering about a mug shot. Act mature and dignified. Notice I said act, because inside you sure won't feel like it. Lie to yourself, wear that mask. Eventually, you will start to believe your own pretence.

- No stalking your ex.
- Avoid, AVOID, **AVOID**!

Similarly, you need to put your foot down if that person insists on hanging around the periphery of your life in an effort to take you on an emotional roller coaster. Roller coaster rides scare the living daylights out of you, and upset your stomach. Get off. Let your caller ID do its job. If he calls simply do not answer. You pay the bill, you can choose if to answer or not. If he tries to get messages to you via friends, put them on notice that they too will be cut off if they persist. If he comes by to "talk" don't let him in. He is no longer welcome. Pretend you aren't home, even if your car is parked out front. Sounds cruel? This is no different from how you treat those Jehovah's Witnesses who come around on Saturday mornings, and they are not the ones who broke your heart. If he sends you flowers, send them back. You need to send a clear, unmistakable message that it is over and you mean it.

Sure, sure you may hear you are being harsh, unfair, stubborn, callous, cold-hearted, selfish and cruel. Listen. Ignore all this hue and cry. When you were together you gave your Ex your all. You were loving, attentive, thoughtful, generous, warm, supportive, faithful. They had the best you could give. Now, you are hurt and suffering and doing all you can to stop the haemorrhaging of your heart. That is your main focus right now. His intrusion into your space is not helping to achieve this. Gently but firmly remind him that it is over between you two and you are not in a position to entertain him right now. No speeches, no explanation, no drama.

You are not obligated to listen to him bemoan and bewail how terrible he feels, how you are hurting him. And you don't owe him anything. **Each of us is responsible for our own feelings.** You are working on getting yours out of the dumps. He needs to go work on his. Suggest that he purchase a copy of this book. For heaven's sake, don't allow him to take you on a guilt trip by bringing up all the wonderful things he did *for* you. That too is all in the past and should be allowed to remain there. If at any time you feel yourself weakening in your resolve to keep that person away, or feel guilty about "what you are doing to him", refresh your memory with all that he did *to* you. An invaluable tool to assist in memorialising your car wreck of a relationship, and keeping you grounded, is explained next.

An Ex refusing to leave you alone, even when repeatedly told to do so, involves what is legally regarded as harassment. The police should be introduced at this stage to explain this concept to him.

- No trespassing.

- No guilt trips.
- Call the authorities if necessary.

Notes

_____
_____
_____
_____
_____
_____
_____
_____
_____
_____
_____
_____
_____
_____
_____
_____
_____
_____
_____
_____
_____
_____
_____
_____

THREE

♥

Transfer

SOMETIMES IT IS over and you have accepted it, but you don't feel that closure you need to move on. You start remembering so many broken promises, words and situations that hurt you, questions you should have asked, things you should have said which, unless resolved, you will not be able to put the matter to rest, to move on. This is the devil. You want to have that conversation, that argument, that telling-off session, because it means you will have contact with the person. And if you still call and talk, no matter how loudly, does it still mean it is really over?

The first few days after Brian and I broke up,
every broken promise, unkind word and unfair

*accusation came flooding back, playing
in my head constantly like a stuck record,
keeping me awake at night. I wanted to call
and remind him of all the sweet things he
had said to me that were now obviously lies.
All the plans we made together that died
when "we" ceased to be. I wanted to let him
know that I saw through his lies, that he was
a fake, that he hurt me and I hated him.*

But instead of confrontation, I suggest that you express any unresolved feelings or issues you may have in the form of a letter to the other party. Writing this letter allows you to **transfer all these pent up, nagging thoughts onto paper**, so you no longer have to walk around with them in your heart and in your head. Write down everything: all the hurt, anger, sadness, suspicions, evidence, and conclusions which contributed to the end. You need not deliver the letter; just put it away somewhere safe.

My letter to Brian went along these lines;

*"Dear Judas Iscariot,
You are indeed the most selfish person I have
ever met. You used to tell me I was too good*

for you, that you didn't deserve me. At the time I thought you were being sweet, but I realise now that you were being honest. After investing two precious, long years of my life in being with you, loving you and fooling myself you loved me in return, it was a stab in the back to be tossed aside because, as you put it, I was 'too demanding and unreasonable'. What were my 'demands'? To be taken out every once in a while? To just once go on a romantic walk on the beach at sunset? And no, going over to your place does not count as "going out".

And 'unreasonable'? Was it unreasonable to expect you to show up on time to the special birthday dinner I prepared for you? Yes, you came, but it was after midnight and you were half-drunk. I hope you and your buddies had a blast.

Oh, but I forgot I was also childish and spoiled. Why? Because I know when I am not wanted? I called you at 4 p.m. and you were watching football. I came over at 8 p.m. and you were still watching football. At 8:30 p.m., after sitting there in silence while you watched football, your phone rang. You proceeded to leave me with the football to go chat in low tones, in the other room, with whomever was on the other end of the line. Why were you surprised to come back to the living room and find me gone?

*Looking back, I question how I could have been such a sucker for punishment, to have tortured myself for two years. You did us both a favour when you left. I hope you find someone who deserves you. I know **now** I deserve much better."*

The objective of this exercise is not to re-open communications with the other party. **The aim is to purge your mind and soul of bitterness.** But if you absolutely must deliver this letter to share the misery you are feeling, please keep a copy. This letter will become crucial later on in the grieving process. You will eventually see why.

Another therapeutic tool I employed when Michael and I agreed to go our separate ways, was art. Now, I am no artist, not by any stretch of the imagination. But after writing the "Dear Judas" letter I still had some built-up emotions inside that needed to be set free. I couldn't scream out loud lest the neighbours got alarmed and called the police (this action is best reserved for lonely hilltops) and I didn't want to throw and break things, because I would have to clean up afterwards.

Instead, I got out a box of crayons and a large piece of blank, new, white paper. As I stood before my canvas, I closed my eyes and remembered Mike. In meandering, lazy lines along the border, I retraced our love story with sweet hazy, pastels. The gentle blue of when we first met; the gay yellows and pinks of the innocent fun and laughter we shared; the peach of sharing our innermost thoughts; a first touch. As I moved closer to the centre of the canvas, next I shaded, using a vibrant green, signifying our growing affection, the bold blue of our love; aqua and violet of our special memories; and in rhythmic circles in the very centre, the deep orange and red of our passion.

But wait! Dark blue and brown, deep, heavy, sharp erratic lines disturb the order and cut through the beauty. Why did you break our date? Why are you now so often late? Why must I always be the one to wait? Deep purple scrawls from top to bottom, left to right. How come your phone is off when you go out with the guys? Now I'm catching you in bolder lies. Who are you messaging constantly when you are with me? What's that on your neck? A foreign hickey? Then black! Your accusations and criticism— "You're too independent! You don't need me! You don't trust me! I called you 'Joyann' accidentally! Didn't I say I was sorry?"

When the frenzy was over and I came back to the present, my canvas was completely black and crumpled, with a large hole in the middle. I stood back and assessed it. A masterpiece! And I felt good.

So write a song; write a poem; paint a mural; create a new board game, tee shirt line or greeting cards for jilted lovers. Turn that bag of lemons you are holding into lemonade, lemon cake, lemon tarts and lemon meringue pie.

Notes

FOUR

Ventilation

IF YOU HAVE friends, true friends, lean on them at this most difficult time. Let them know you are hurting and you need their support, love and encouragement. **A problem shared is a problem halved**. Meet up with them and go shopping for a new outfit or to see a movie. Do not sit around the house in his old tee shirt, eating everything in your refrigerator, drinking the entire bottle of wine by yourself, wallowing in misery. Go out and get some sunshine on your face, get some fresh air.

As much as I recommend your reaching out to a few trusted friends for support at this time, be reasonable. While you were with "Mr Wrong", is it possible that these friends may have been neglected and may still be a bit annoyed at being ignored? Don't pressure them to fill up all of your empty life. Limit the number of these friends to two (2) and keep your exchanges as dignified as possible. Do not call them when, for example, you are in the full throes of a crying fit, or if you find it difficult to share without breaking down. Not all friends can handle these messy scenes and may be unsure of what to say or do to help. So they may resort to avoiding your calls if they know each conversation ends with you bawling out his name and yelling "Whhhhhyyyyyy!!!!" Try not to overburden these friends. Calling them five or more times a day to discuss "it" (break-up) and "him" (the culprit), is unacceptable. They have their own problems too. And for goodness sake, do not call them late at night when you feel lonely. Remember: A friend in need can be a pain in the butt.

There is an old saying that goes, "Don't speak ill of the dead." Similarly, "**Do not speak ill of your dead relationship.**" As you go about your daily life, it is inevitable that you will run into someone who knows you and your (former) partner and naturally, they will ask after them. Some, innocently, out of genuine interest and politeness, and others because they may have heard the news about the break-up and want the sordid details right from the horse's mouth.

Tempting as it may be, do not go into a diatribe about what a lying, domestic animal the person was. Or how many times he cheated on you, how much money he borrowed and never repaid or how much his feet stank. This repetition of details for all and sundry does not in any way elevate you in their eyes as a saint for having put up with this treatment. Quite the opposite. It makes them wonder what sort of idiot you were for dating such a loser, or it sounds pathetic that you would allow someone to treat you like a doormat and then be dumped. Retelling the story also keeps it alive and in the present. The exact opposite of what we are trying to achieve.

Instead, when asked, "How is Jimmy?" your reply is, "We are no longer in touch." If the person persists and asks, "Really? How come?" your reply should be, "Things did not work out." Full stop. If questioned further, repeat this answer. They will soon get the message that it is none of their business and you do not wish to discuss it. Let them dig somewhere else for their dirt. This answer is in no way rude. **You must protect your borders from trespassers, enemies and spies.**

- No rehashing of details.
- Protect your borders.

I caution against sharing your pain with too many "friends" for good reason. Not all of them may have genuine intentions where you are concerned. Some may even be secretly happy about the demise of your relationship. Maybe you neglected them, or maybe they secretly hated your partner or were jealous of your relationship. These persons are usually the ones who goad you into rehashing all the gory details, examining every fragment without offering any useful advice or encouragement. Any interest they may have in your current situation may be only morbid curiosity. These "friends" are poisonous. They may take delight in tossing the fragments of your torn life into the wind and who knows where the pieces may end up. Maybe directly in enemy territory, at the feet of the last person you need to know about your emotional collapse- your Ex.

Here is a further word of caution. You may think that if your former lover knew how poorly you were doing without him he might come back to you. This hardly ever happens. Do you want his pity or to make him feel guilty? Would this help you heal in any way? I doubt it. Knowing you are a pitiful mess may actually bolster his ego. Do you really want that?

A final word on friends: Please, do not for a moment believe that the Ex's friends are your friends. Even friends you made as a couple may slowly back away and run for the hills when catastrophe strikes your union. After all, break-ups are contagious, and now that you are single and available, you are no longer a friend, you are a threat. Know well in advance who your true friends are. If you don't have any close friends, or for whatever reason you find yourself alone at this time, please keep reading.

And while we are discussing emotional collapse, let's take time to chat about what is potentially your most valuable resource– crying, and potentially your most damaging– self-pity. They are both a very natural part of the grieving process. **So cry. It is therapeutic**. Cry loud, cry long, cry till your eyes are red and swollen and your nose becomes blocked. **But cry in private.** You need to hold on to whatever self-esteem you have left. You don't need anybody's pity. During my period of mourning, I maintained the following crying schedule:

- Twice a day for one week – Once in the morning and again at bedtime.
- Once a day for one week – Either in the morning or at bedtime, depending on when I felt weakest.
- Once a week for four weeks – Saturday afternoons, or whenever I felt loneliest.
- Never again.

Make a strong effort not to exceed this very generous dosage so as not to become dependent. And if you need less than prescribed, more power to you. Allow yourself only one day of self-pity per week. This too will become increasingly unnecessary.

> I remember vividly a particularly sad morning after Robert and I called it quits. I had stopped by the convenience store to grab some breakfast before going to work.

Consumed by grief and feeling particularly low, I somehow still managed to notice something strange going on with the cashier. As I got to the front of the line with my purchases, I realised she was cashing and crying, making change and crying, bagging and crying. Her colleague was admonishing her for taking "his" call and letting "him" upset her, something she had been previously warned not to do. This cashier had not cut the cord. Face to face with someone obviously in the same position as I was, made me feel encouraged for two reasons. 1 I was not alone. Somebody else was suffering as I was. 2. I was doing much better than she. At least I was holding it together in public.

- Talk it out.
- Cry it out.
- Cry in carefully measured doses.
- Go easy on the self-pity.

Notes

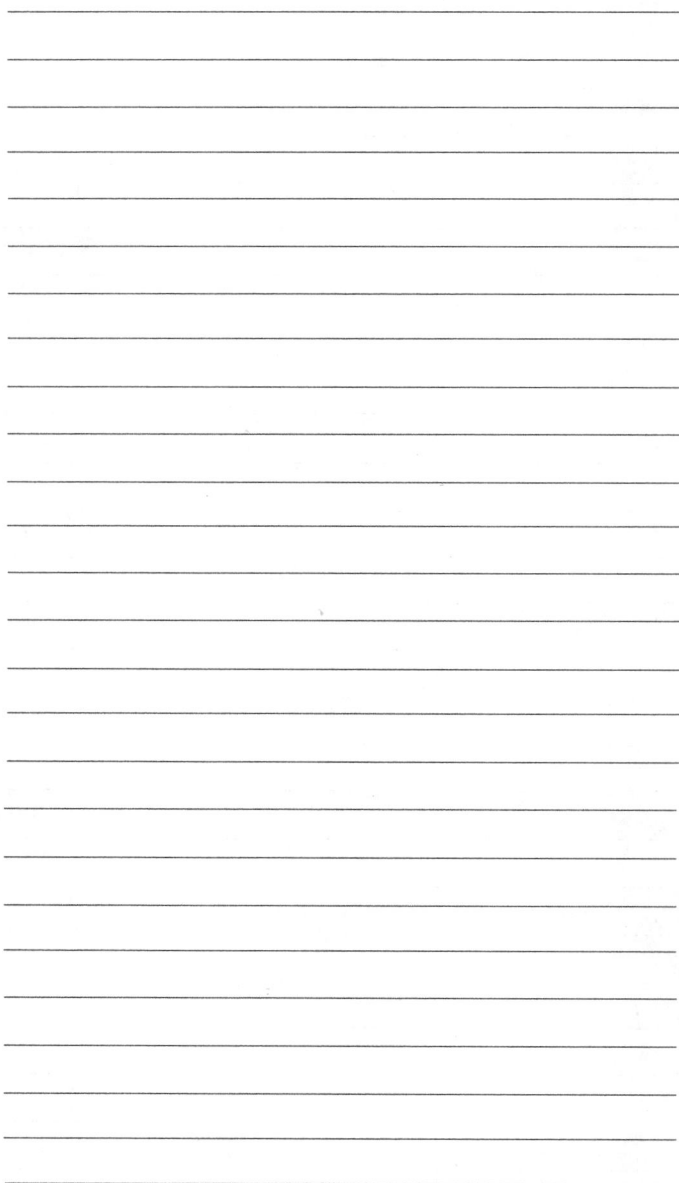

FIVE

Stumbling Blocks

I NOW WISH to mention three very dangerous practices we sometimes erroneously believe are beneficial to our healing, but in fact are not helpful at all, often making our lives more miserable instead.

Stumbling Block #1:
Listening to the wrong type of music

We have all heard that "music has charms to soothe a savage breast", so at this time in your recovery, it is very important what types of songs you listen to. I know it seems the natural thing to do, but now is not the time to listen to sappy love songs about heartbreak, love-loss, betrayal or revenge. And the most destructive song of all is the song you and your former someone declared to be "Our Song". This song must be banned from your playlist. Such songs will only serve to make you cry excessively, which can completely throw you off your 'crying schedule'. You are already mortally wounded. You don't need to be made to feel any worse.

Songs like: *Un-Break My Heart* – Toni Braxton; *Don't Leave Me* – Black Street; *I'll Die Without You* – PM Dawn; *I Can't Live if Living is Without You* – Mariah Carey; *Almost Doesn't Count* – Brandi, are all guaranteed to leave you bawling your guts out in the shower, into your pillow, on your living room floor, in your car.

A word of caution about crying in the car. Make sure you pull off the road if you cannot get home in time. It is very difficult to see where you are going with tears in your eyes, thus making you become a hazard to yourself and other road users.

Instead, I recommend listening to strong songs, encouraging songs, uplifting songs, happy songs, empowering songs, praise party songs. Here are a few of my favourites when the bottom fell out of my relationships:

- *I Will Survive* – Gloria Gaynor;
- *I'm Every Woman* – Whitney Houston & Chaka Khan;
- *Survivor* –Destiny's Child;
- *Not Gon' Cry* – Mary J Blige;
- *New Attitude* – Patti LaBelle.

An even better idea is writing a break-up song, like Adele's *Set Fire to the Rain* or Sam's Smith *I'm Not the Only One*. Making millions of dollars from a break-up number one hit song would be the sweetest revenge of all.

Stumbling Block #2:
The Rebound Relationship

No matter how long or short your relationship was, the exit of your significant other from your life will definitely create a void. The morning wakeup call; the 'good night, sleep tight, I love you' message; once a month lunch date; Friday night dinners; Saturday night movies; bank holiday picnics; Christmas family gatherings; the "plus one" at wedding receptions and parties; ball games and limes–all no more. Suddenly, you have a lot more spare time on your hands and you absolutely hate it! (Don't despair, there will be ample opportunity to redeem the time you lost when you had to compromise and sacrifice for the sake of being a couple.)

Regardless of how tempting it may be, especially on those lonely, rainy nights, **now is the worst time to start a new relationship.** Your emotions are too raw and your judgement is not to be trusted.

I still feel much guilt and regret when I think of Dominic. Such a kind, sweet, tender, loving soul, whose heart I completely crushed. I was tired and emotionally drained after the drawn out ending of my saga with Dwayne finally closed. Starved for affection and appreciation, I hastily turned to Dominic for solace. I showered him with affection that had remained unused and unappreciated for months. Inevitably, Dominic became totally infatuated with me and declared his love. It was unfortunate that I did not realise before then that I was not that into him. He pleaded with me to explain why I no longer wanted to see him, but what could I say? I only just realised that I have been using you to boost my self-confidence and get over my feelings for my Ex"? Indeed not! I still feel very ashamed whenever I bump into him. Thankfully, this is a rare event.

I learned the hard way that getting involved with a distraction and trying to change it into a relationship, will only cause you more pain. And pain is what you are trying to get rid of. Remember–**hurting people, hurt people**.

Stumbling Block #3: Wandering Thoughts

Another pitfall along the pathway to emotional wholeness is useless, wayward, rambling, obsessive, negative, unproductive thoughts: replaying "The End" in your mind, those last words spoken, the last fight, the last goodbye. **Stop these nagging thoughts in their tracks** before they consume your mind. Before they get stuck in your head, like that song you don't like but still catch yourself singing all day. These thoughts only serve to make you sad. You may also find yourself reminiscing about all the good times, thereby elevating the failed relationship to "match made in heaven" status, and putting your Ex up on a pedestal as "the best". Remember the bad times as well. They also happened, and were most likely the reason why the relationship ended. At times like these when your memory becomes cloudy and selective, get out that "Dear Judas" letter and meditate on it. Read, Relive, Remember. This refocusing will quickly bring you back to earth and keep you focused on your goal- Happiness.

- Refrain from listening to sad love songs.
- Now is not the time to start something new.
- Take control of your thoughts.

Having touched on the subject of heaven a moment ago, if you believe nothing that I have told you so far, believe this: Do not discount the power and healing to be found in calling on your Heavenly Father to guide you out of this wilderness; this dry, barren desert; this shadowy valley of death.

Pray and pray hard. Pray every day. Pray several times a day. Pray that the hurt and pain will stop. Pray that the love you have for the individual will dry up and be replaced with a feeling of freedom and peace. **God answers prayer.** I also recommend that you attend church during this time, especially if you feel you have lost your will to live. **You need to be around happy people right now**, and there are no happier people I have observed, than Christians in church on Sunday mornings.

I remember one such Sunday after I gave Chris his walking papers. My morning dose of crying had left me particularly empty, so I put on my Sunday best and headed off to a church in my area. Christians love visitors and I was shown to my seat with all the smiles and welcomes and admiring side looks from a few "brothers" to warm my heart and boost my confidence. The worship started off slow and soothing. The melodious and passionate voices accompanied by the skilful musicians invoked God's presence, and I was swept along with the eager flock, into the Throne Room. Suddenly, the atmosphere changed. The tempo of the drums picked up, tambourines were awakened and the heat of the praises being sent up to heaven activated *heaven's sprinkler system, and the blessings showered down like rain. Just the refreshment my thirsty soul was so desperate for. I gazed around like a mesmerised spectator at a magic show. Feet tapping and head bobbing involuntarily, while all around me, brothers and sisters offered up songs of adoration and thanks, dancing and waving their hands. Uninhibited. In the presence of God there is indeed liberty. Freedom to lay down your burdens and smile a while.*

When your situation looks bleak and the days are long and difficult, **encourage yourself**. Tell yourself that this too shall pass, and believe this to be true. Acknowledge your feelings but don't dwell on them. You will get over it, and soon. Believe it. Replace any negative thoughts with more constructive ones, like a weight loss plan, healthy eating plan, self-improvement plan, something beneficial.

Even though you are hurting deeply at this time and just want the pain to stop, it is counter-productive to start any bad habits in an attempt to dull or mask the pain. Smoking, excessive alcohol consumption, illegal drug use and legal drug misuse, over-eating, sleeping around- all of these activities are just temporary fixes, and eventually the pain returns. And now on top of all that, you may have acquired another problem, a possible addiction, a virus, or ten extra pounds. Use this break as an opportunity to invest in yourself and discover your immense strength, creativity, loveliness and magnificence.

- Pray.
- Encourage yourself.
- Believe.

Notes

SIX

When to Seek
Professional Help

ADMITTEDLY, sometimes despite your bravest efforts to get past the hurt, after a month or two you may still not notice any significant improvement, or may even start to feel sadder.

If you are:

- Still crying multiple times a day, every day;
- Not getting any rest at night;
- Tired all day;
- Unable to function at all in your everyday activities;
- Unable to make it out of bed most days;
- Neglecting your personal hygiene;

- Not eating or have started over-indulging;
- Developing any addictive, self-injurious or other negative behaviours;
- Harbouring fantasies of harming yourself or that other person;
- Stalking your Ex;
- Harassing them online, on the phone, or in person;
- Engaging in confrontational, aggressive, threatening or violent behaviour

Then it is time to seek professional help. There is absolutely no shame in this, although you need not advertise it either if you don't want to. **This is your business.** Had you attended your physician with an infection in an intimate area you would not have announced it either, but the visit would have been just as necessary and just as beneficial.

When Mark and I split up it was the full stop at the end of a short but intense drama. The hot bliss of our passionate beginning, ripe with possibilities of a bright and shiny future together, soon became tarnished by harsh words, neglect, betrayal, rejection and abandonment. The sad end of two people who had only one thing in common. I loved Mark and Mark loved Mark too. The end left me very hurt and angry. I did all that I knew how to pick up the pieces and move on, but months later the hurt and anger still felt fresh, like yesterday. He still occupied my every thought. I slept a lot to escape from my pain only to encounter him in my nightmares. I was growing more wretched and bitter each day. I longed for a larger than life eraser so I could just rub him out of existence. I cursed the day I ever laid eyes on him. I only found comfort and pleasure in my fantasies of doing him grievous bodily harm. It was time for therapy.

How do you find a therapist? You can either check your telephone directory and make a random selection for a therapist in a location convenient to you; you can do like me and get a referral from your General Practitioner; or you can ask a trusted friend if they know of someone. Maybe they can even accompany you to the first session for moral support, if you desire. But by all means **do not remain where you are**. As Winston Churchill is quoted as saying, *"If you're going through hell, keep going."* Eventually you will come out on the other side into sunshine.

- Get professional help if you need to.
- Stay the course, keep going.

Notes

SEVEN

Managing Your Stress

WEBMD-Stress Management Health Centre, an online medical resource, defines stress as *"The body's reaction to harmful situations- whether they are real or perceived"*. The article further states *"Stress can affect all aspects of your life, including your emotions, behaviour, thinking ability and physical health."* According to WebMD, stress is brought about by trying to cope with challenging circumstances including work, family members, finances, or relationships. The article also suggests that stress can have both physical and emotional symptoms.

The Physical Symptoms of stress include:

- Low energy
- Headaches
- Upset stomach including diarrhoea, constipation and nausea
- Aches, pain and tense muscles
- Chest pain and rapid heartbeat
- Insomnia
- Frequent colds and infections due to lowered immune response
- Loss of sexual desire and/or ability
- Nervousness and shaking
- Dry mouth and difficulty swallowing
- Clenched jaw and grinding teeth

The Emotional Symptoms of stress include:
- Becoming easily agitated, frustrated and moody
- Feeling overwhelmed, like you are losing control
- Having difficulty relaxing and quieting your mind
- Feeling badly about yourself (low self-esteem), lonely, worthless, depressed
- Avoiding others

During this time of emotional heartache you may experience a few, or even all of the above symptoms of stress. This is all part of the grieving process. But be careful, it can be oh so tempting to lie in bed all day, with your "blanket" of depression and hurt keeping you warm and reassured. If left unchecked, this same "blanket" often times wraps itself tighter and tighter around your body, makes its way up and over your shoulders, past your neck and eventually covers your entire face, threatening to smother the very life out of you. Don't surrender to these feelings. You need not resign yourself to your suffering. Speak to your doctor. He or she will be happy to recommend a course of treatment specifically tailored to alleviate your symptoms.

- Don't suffer needlessly.
- Medical intervention is at your disposal.

In addition to your doctor's advice, here are a few of my suggestions to help you climb and conquer Heartbreak Mountain.

Get Out!

At all costs, get out of the house!!!

I firmly believe that the reason why we so often feel that the world is spinning out of control is because we are constantly being bombarded by too much information. Back when life was simpler, news came on the radio three times a day and once on TV at night. Meals were cooked at home on a stove, and no matter how hungry you were, you had to wait till it was finished. Speed limits were lower and people actually spoke to each other, often, and face to face. Nowadays it is instant messaging, posting, blogging, instagramming, emailing. Business can be conducted 24 hours a day and news updates from every corner of the globe can be had every minute. Emails are received in voluminous amounts. It can be truly stressful and overwhelming. A mind already overwhelmed by heartache can hardly stand up to the pressure of this information overload. It is well worth it for an hour or so every day, just to come out from under the pile of electronic nuisance devices and reconnect with nature. Don't forget, we as human beings are also part of nature.

So get out and notice a weed growing defiantly through a crack in the sidewalk; a bird diligently searching in the grass for some morsel; an ant valiantly carrying a huge crumb with ease; a butterfly flirting with a beautiful flower; the clouds making and unmaking interesting shapes; the smell of the earth after a shower of rain; the reviving freshness of a cool breeze as it brushes past your skin; a sunset with all the hues and colours it transfigures into as the sun disappears; the first flickering star of the evening; a spine-tingling, awe-inspiring full moon; all the blues and greens of the ocean along with its smell and sounds and the sand between your toes; birds flying overhead in perfect formation; the intricate design of a spider's web; lambs leaping and butting each other, attacking playfully. All these exciting things are still happening right outside your door. Leave the smart phone on silent, or better yet, at home. Go out and become part of the picture. Take some crumbs along; you may make a few friends.

Nature not your thing? Go to the movies, walk around the mall, catch up on your reading, volunteer for a special project at work, join a gym, visit family. Go to places your Ex never wanted to go: a music recital, the theatre, the museum, a wine tasting, and art exhibition, open mike night at a jazz club. Just get out! Don't stay in the house moping and don't start any bad habits (smoking, drinking, over-eating, candy crush on Facebook). Take up a new, exciting, unusual or neglected hobby. Explore a new interest. Not only will this help you to pass the time but you may discover a latent talent. The added bonus of doing something new is that you will meet new people and make new friends. Take up painting, dancing, photography, writing, yoga, rock climbing, hiking, ceramic tiling, swimming, a French class, a cooking class. None of these activities requires a partner and all are positive ways to redirect your focus and energy.

> When Frank ran off with Janelle my self-esteem plummeted. Frustrated and unable to sleep, I took up a hoe and very early every morning, busied myself in the front yard removing every invading blade of grass and unwanted bush. After there was nothing else to chop, I took up walking and eventually running as exercise. I was never in such good shape.

Don't discount the value of physical activity.

The energy and hormones released are natural mood lifters.

Escape!

Sometimes getting out of the house is not far enough. You may need to get further away from the wreckage.

Liam, Liam – forever etched on my heart. We were college sweethearts our future spread out before us like a soft fluffy carpet strewn with rose petals, lighted by scented candles and accented with chocolate-covered strawberries. Handsome and intelligent, intriguing, witty, sensitive. The long and shiny knife plunged deep into my heart when he finally broke down and admitted that all my suspicions and accusations were correct. With tears streaming down his face, he blubbered some apology that had come too late. I was staring into the face of a complete stranger. Who was this person, this crumpled, repulsive heap, and where was my true love, the man I dreamt of marrying and bearing his children (names for whom I had already chosen)? In the instant of his admission, the backdrop of my picture-perfect life, our perfect love, ripped and fell away, exposing the bare ugly empty stage of truth. I remembered thinking, "It was all fake. Everything was a lie..." Take a bow Liam. Part well played. And all this mess right before final exams too. How inconvenient. I did not have time for a nervous breakdown. God held me up and brought me through. God is not a man.

A week or two after final exams, my best girlfriend and I took a trip to a Caribbean island. Exploring the volcano, the sulphur springs, the food, the shopping, the night life, single for the first time in years. It was refreshing and freeing to mingle with the locals, flirt and thoroughly enjoy my experience knowing that my actions were not hurting anybody. The change of scenery and making new friends were like balm to my wounded soul.

A change of scenery is highly recommended, especially after a long-term union goes south.

There are too many memories everywhere, all around, in every corner. Time away takes you out of your usual routine, into the less familiar. Away from the graveyard where you laid your relationship to rest and back onto the main street of life, creating new memories as you go, which do not include the dearly departed.

A change in scenery proved helpful some years later post-Steve. This time I headed off to the big city to spend a few weeks with my favourite cousin and meet up with some old school friends I hadn't seen in years. The sights, the hustle and bustle of everyday life, the shopping, ole talking into the wee hours. In no time at all my cousin had given me a makeover- my wardrobe updated, make up perfected, spirits lifted. I hardly thought about what's-his-name the whole time I was there.

Unable to take a couple weeks off at this time or finances do not allow you to go far away? Check into a local hotel for a few nights. Avail yourself of the pool, restaurant and spa. The fluffy white towels, mini bar and cable TV and remote controlled by you. Still too steep? Volunteer to house sit for a friend who may be going out of town or spend a weekend visiting a family member who you have been promising to visit for a long time.

Oh! Before you leave for your trip, I highly recommend you make a few changes at home. Re-arrange the furniture, paint your bedroom in a cool calming colour, change your drapes, mount that print you bought ages ago but never got around to hanging, put away your everyday plates and glasses and put out the ones reserved for guests. Buy place mats, new pillows and comforter, shower curtain and mats, the girlier the better. Get new covers for your throws or turn the old covers inside out. Get a fake house plant. Do as much or as little as your budget allows. After your time away, you will return to your "new" home. Ahhhh. The change will do you loads of good. No bad memories here!

Affirm!

Affirm yourself every day. Sit down and write a list of all your positive attributes and strengths, the qualities you love about yourself as well as those highly valued and appreciated by others. Every morning start your day with a prayer of thanks to God for allowing you to see another day. You are down, not dead, so give thanks for that. Next, look in the mirror and with your list of attributes in hand, read out loud the first three attributes. Repeat three times. For example, "I am intelligent; I am beautiful, I am creative". The next morning focus on the next three on the list. When you complete your list, start from the beginning again. You may feel silly doing this at first, but don't worry, nobody is watching or listening. Feel confident repeating your positives. After all, they are all true and you will start to feel better about yourself.

Speaking these truths to yourself each day builds you up, boosts your confidence and equips you to go out and live life boldly. Switch your personal soundtrack from, *Ain't no sunshine when she's gone* - Bill Withers, to *I can see clearly now the rain is gone* - Johnny Nash/Jimmy Cliff. Of course you may not feel this way yet, but your rainbow is there, only temporarily obscured by a few pesky clouds. Add uplifting songs like Yolanda Adam's *Victory* or Papa San's *Higher Heights*, to your playlist.

When was the last time you had a professional portrait done? Photograph, oil or water colour-it doesn't matter. Make sure it is highly flattering, embellished if necessary. Hang your portrait in a prominent place. If you are artistic, even if only slightly, hang your own masterpieces on the walls. Admit it. You have seen worse pieces parading as art.

Indulge!

It is accepted that emotional pain and stress lower the body's resistance to illness and can trigger psychosomatic conditions like migraines and stomach aches, exacerbated no doubt by your poor eating and sleep habits, muscle tension and depression. At this delicate time I advise that you:

- Pamper yourself. A LOT.

Get your hair done, nails, facial, massage, or just give yourself an at-home pedicure every Friday, using the most outrageous nail colours you can find. Indulge yourself in nightly baths or showers surrounded by scented candles. Nothing is too good for you. You are going through a rough time right now and you need gentleness and lots of love.

If you are brave enough, try something different with your hair. Different, not drastic. Carefree not crazy. Add or subtract, straighten or curl, colour or highlight, all in the name of change. Nourish your body with fresh healthy foods. Get plenty of rest, sunshine, fresh air and exercise, and drink lots of water, as crying leaves you dehydrated. Your body will thank you.

> Every Friday night was foot spa night. Warm water infused with oils or soothing salts drew the tension and tiredness from my weary feet. And each Friday a new nail colour, the bolder the better. The last Saturday of every month was also eagerly anticipated as it was set aside for my sojourns to the massage therapist. With a master's skill he relaxed and released tension and tightness from muscles I never knew I had. I always left his care, feeling I was floating on a cloud of air, surrounded by joy, peace and tranquillity.

Dress Up!

How you look on the outside affects how you feel on the inside. So dress well, smell nice, hold your head high and smile. Update your wardrobe with a few tasteful pieces. Go outside your comfort zone and you may surprise yourself at what you discover. Apply a bit of makeup to enhance your more flattering features. Please, no clown makeup. Some women feel totally alive and confident in a new pair of shoes, a power suit or sexy lingerie. Buy a new outfit, handbag, shoes or earrings, but do not overspend. You do not need any more problems, like debt, right now.

In looking your best you will make others believe that you are feeling fine and soon enough you will also "fool" yourself. Besides, how can you feel less than fabulous with all the compliments you are receiving and heads you are turning? Looking your best at all times is vital because you never know when you may run into "someone". They must never think that you are suffering. Give the impression that your life has greatly improved since they left. Give a polite nod of recognition and a smile or a cheery hello, and walk away, strutting your stuff. You score double points if he happens to be with "anyone". Don't feel jealous. Seeing you looking gorgeous and confident will strike fear into her heart and doubts into his.

How they choose to handle their feelings on encountering this veritable goddess is really none of your business.

Reach Out!

Take the focus off yourself and your present circumstances by reaching out and helping others, by doing volunteer work or just everyday kind deeds. Join a local community, youth or church group in your area. Help out at a soup kitchen. Read to the residents in a retirement home. Walk your neighbour's dog. This will give you a great feeling of self-worth.

For two years I volunteered my Saturday mornings on the paediatric ward at the hospital. It started out as my shameless effort to score points with God. Of all the things I was doing wrong, I hoped helping to care for his little ones, even in such a small way, might make Him more inclined to hear my prayers. But spending time with those sick children was such a great inspiration to me. Never complaining, but instead making themselves happy despite their circumstances. The minor setback in my love life was miniscule compared to what some of these little ones were bravely battling every day. I read stories, sang to and fed, and sometimes just chatted with these gems, anything to distract them from their discomfort if only for a while. It was an honour and inspiration to serve them.

Look Up!

Let me introduce you to the most important tool in your arsenal. Your daily devotions. So get out your Bible or buy one if you've lost it. Read the Psalms (not the angry ones about God smiting your enemies), the ones about God's forgiveness and His love—true love, real love, undying love, healing love. Receive this love. This is love that can be trusted. Through your daily Bible reading you will discover and connect to your Heavenly Father and discover the wonderful, marvellous, awesome, generous, loving, trustworthy, caring God that He is. God never lied to you, used you, misled you, or broke promises He made to you. Make him number one in your life, as He should be, as He deserves to be. God loves you, and is interested in you. He wants to help you, so let Him. Meditate on the truths to be found in His word. Can't get to sleep? Read a love letter from God. Hurting and think no one cares? Tell God how you feel. No fancy words are necessary. Tears are a language He understands.

In some of my darkest hours I was particularly strengthened by these two verses in the book of Romans:

> *"For I am convinced that neither death nor life, neither angels nor demons, neither the present nor the future, nor any powers, neither height nor depth, nor anything else in all creation, will be able to separate us from the love of God that is in Christ Jesus our Lord."*- Romans 8:38-39 NIV.

Memorise a verse or two that you can call on in times of sadness, hopelessness, desperation, doubt or disappointment. Repeat it over and over to yourself, out loud in the mirror, or in your head. My favourite was, and still is Numbers 23:19:

"God is not a man, that He should lie, nor a son of man that He should change His mind. Does He speak and then not act? Does He promise and not fulfil?" NIV

Mending broken hearts is God's specialty. You don't believe me? Check out the book of Isaiah.

"The Spirit of the Lord God is upon me, because the Lord has anointed me to preach good tidings to the poor, He has sent Me to heal the broken hearted, to proclaim liberty to the captives, and the opening of the prison to those who are bound, To proclaim the acceptable year of the Lord and the day of vengeance to our God; to comfort all who mourn, to console those who mourn in Zion. To give them beauty for ashes, the oil of joy for mourning, the garment of praise for the spirit of heaviness; that they may be called trees of righteousness, the planting of the Lord that He may be glorified." Isaiah 61:1-3 NKJV

Know that in your darkest hour you are blessed.

"Blessed are they that mourn for they shall be comforted." Matthew 5:4 NKJV

Receive the freedom to be found in His presence and the abundant life He offers.

"Now the Lord is the Spirit, and where the Spirit of the Lord is there is liberty." 2 Corinthians 3:17 NKJV.

"The thief does not come except to steal, and to kill and to destroy. I have come that they may have life, and that they may have it more abundantly." John 10:10 NKJV

In closing, I encourage you to be kind to yourself. Kind but firm. Allow yourself to be sad but don't wallow in self-pity, no matter how warm and comforting it may feel. There will be good days, and there will be bad days. Rejoice in the good days and enjoy them fully. On the bad days, look forward to the good days ahead. Increasingly, there will be more and more good days in a row. You had a life before this person and you will have a life again. Most of all, know that you will conquer this heartbreak.

Notes

Bibliography

Review of General Psychology, Boutwell, Dr
  Brian. Page 24. http://www.dailymail.
  co.uk/health/article-3013254/You-
  recover-heartbreak-Scientists-discover-
  humans-hardwired-overcome-rejection.
  html#ixzz3pPIp978n

WebMD. Stress Management Health Centre,
  Page 63. http://www.webmd.com/balance/
  stress-management/default.htm